New England Anti-Slavery Convention

Tributes to Theodore Parker

New England Anti-Slavery Convention

Tributes to Theodore Parker

ISBN/EAN: 9783337407988

Printed in Europe, USA, Canada, Australia, Japan

Cover: Foto ©Thomas Meinert / pixelio.de

More available books at **www.hansebooks.com**

TRIBUTES

TO

THEODORE PARKER,

COMPRISING THE

EXERCISES AT THE MUSIC HALL.

ON SUNDAY, JUNE 17, 1860,

WITH THE

PROCEEDINGS

OF THE

NEW ENGLANI ANTI-SLAVERY CONVENTION,

AT THE MELODEON, MAY 31,

AND THE

RESOLUTIONS OF THE FRATERNITY AND THE TWENTY-
EIGHTH CONGREGATIONAL SOCIETY.

———

BOSTON:
PUBLISHED BY THE FRATERNITY.
1860.

COMMEMORATIVE EXERCISES

THE MUSIC HALL.

EXERCISES in commemoration of the death of the late
REVEREND THEODORE PARKER, were held by the Twenty-
Eighth Congregational Society, in the Music Hall, on Sunday, June 17th. The capacious hall was crowded to reple-
tion in every part, and many remained standing through the
entire services, which lasted upwards of two hours.

Among the most strongly marked characteristics of Mr.
Parker was a love of flowers. This extended almost to a
passion. It was therefore in the highest degree proper, and
also beautifully suggestive, that on this occasion there
should be a floral tribute. Accordingly the altar at which
he was wont to preach was literally covered with flowers,
tastefully and elegantly arranged—the spontaneous gift of
many friends of Mr. Parker. In front of the altar was sus-
pended a CROSS composed of white roses and evergreen.
On each side were numerous wreaths of variegated flowers,
the rarest and most beautiful of the season ; and upon the
top at each wing were bouquets large in size, placed in
vases. Close beside the Bible, was the favorite of Mr.
Parker, the Lily of the Valley.

The exercises were commenced with a Voluntary upon the organ, which was succeeded by the following Chant by the choir :

CHANT FROM PSALM CXXXIX.

O Lord, thou hast searched me and known me. Thou knowest my down-sitting and mine up-rising, thou understandest my thoughts afar off. Thou compassest my path and my lying down, and art acquainted with all my ways. For there is not a word in my tongue, but lo, O Lord, thou knowest it altogether. Whither shall I go from thy spirit, or whither shall I flee from thy presence ? If I ascend up into heaven, thou art there; if I make my bed in hell, behold thou art there. If I take the wings of the morning, and dwell in the uttermost parts of the sea; even there shall thy hand lead me and thy right hand shall hold me. If I say, Surely the darkness shall cover me, even the night shall be light about me. Yea, the darkness hideth not from thee, but the night shineth as the day: the darkness and the light are both alike to thee. How precious also are thy thoughts unto me, O God, how great is the sum of them. If I should count them they are more in number than the sand : when I awake, I am still with thee. Search me, O God, and know my heart: try me and know my thoughts : And see if there be any wicked way in me, and lead me in the way everlasting.

A fervent and impressive prayer was then offered by Rev. John L. Russell of Salem. Mr. Russell dwelt upon the great loss which the Society and the world now experienced in the death of Mr. Parker. He alluded touchingly to the sorrow of the surviving partner and family relatives, and lamented the incompletion of his great labors; and concluded by imploring that the sad event might inspire

all who grieved his departure, to an increased activity and
zeal in those principles and works to the carrying out of
which he had sacrificed his life.

The choir then sung the following hymn, which, together
with the other hymns, and the passages from the Scriptures,
had been selected by Mr. Parker for this occasion, several
months previous to his death.

HYMN 95.

WHILE Thee I seek, protecting Power,
  Be my vain wishes stilled !
And may this consecrated hour
  With better hopes be filled.

Thy love the powers of thought bestowed ;
  To Thee my thoughts would soar ;
Thy mercy o'er my life has flowed ;
  That mercy I adore !

In each event of life how clear
  Thy ruling hand I see !
Each blessing to my soul more dear,
  Because conferred by Thee.

In every joy that crowns my days,
  In every pain I bear,
My heart shall find delight in praise,
  Or seek relief in prayer.

When gladness wings my favored hour,
  Thy love my thoughts shall fill ;
Resigned, when storms of sorrow lower,
  My soul shall meet thy will.

My lifted eye, without a tear,
  The gathering storm shall see ;
My steadfast heart shall know no fear ;
  That heart shall rest on Thee.

1 *

Friends: I *must* speak; but least of that of which my heart is full. I knew Mr. Parker well from the time of his going to West Roxbury. In his last letter to me, he writes, "There has never been a day since I left home that I have not often thought of your father and his dear ones. He is one of my oldest friends. His is the last house I was ever in at home except my own." Again that trembling hand wrote; but the mortal eye of that friend, the first to welcome him there and here, was not to read the written words. That friend had gone, I trust to welcome him again. Would that I could venture to try to pay tribute due to the friendship of so many years. But the day of his first illness, and that of his death, the very hymn he chose, which we have just sung, open such recent sorrows and quick associations, that I must turn away, with one glance, from old memories of his house at Spring street, over which the pines were always whispering; his library there, where that great soul was trained, mastering tools wherewith to do the work of the world, and the fair garden on which it looked; of his love for all without, within; of the village church, with its silent finger and its little band; the Sabbath school; of Brook Farm, where we lived — its woods and fields, and stream of gold and gems, dearer and fairer in the pictures which the child, the boy, daguerreotypes, than the poet or romancer can make them; of the old home — of the strolls there; of communion with minds of the past and the present there opened; and altogether from later and fresher things, for they would lead to that of which I could not speak.

I remember, even before that, how his stalwart frame swept along the avenues of Divinity Hall. I remember the manner of his early preaching. In that was shown what I always thought the chief element of his character and source of his power. He was often utterly overcome by emotion; his utterance choked; tears flowed; his frame shook. It was beyond what was natural, even at that age. He has told us that "he preached only what he had himself experienced." Gigantic as his developed intellect became — great as were the treasures of learning he diffused — his greatest power was the native impulse of his soul — his affectional nature. No mind, no learning could express it. Though to the world they seemed solid as the ground, they only floated on its bosom.

Born on soil sacred to Freedom — of stock culled in England, and trained for two centuries in the best physical and moral culture of the world — himself reared in schools not the costliest, but the best — taught the love of labor, self-reliance, absolute reverence for God and conscience — he surprised the world by the intellect that embraced the will that moved it. But these only beat with the impulses of his mighty heart. I do not wish to vindicate all. But as the dust of earth shall fall, this element will justify much that is questioned now. He did not believe in calling black white. Let time and truth judge his sayings. What he spoke in love will live. Do you not remember how, in his discourse on Adams — when the building shook, and his voice was silenced as the ice and snow fell with the shock of an earthquake before the sun of Spring — he wished it so with the character he was discussing — with what joy he reviewed the glorious labors of the long Indian summer of that life, the rapture with which he hailed its closing act, summed up in that Saxon sentence, "the great loud *No* of an old man going home to his God?" Is the wail of a true heart over powers perverted — the "*woe*" of him who speaks in the cause of Humanity and God, to those who smite what they might save — to be condemned?

The Resolve "that Theodore Parker *should* have a chance to be heard" was more than the word of a friend, or a protest for religious freedom, or a plan for a free church. Before the South Boston sermon, it was known who and what was coming in this young preacher, who had said: "God still lives — man has lost none of his high nature;" and in his parable of Paul: "I shall walk by God's light, and fear not." It was thought that the *new truth* would be spread by his voice; perhaps not dreamed that one man could spread it so widely. But that simple Resolve, the seed of this Society, was dropped in faith that that truth would prevail — the mover of it having a year or two before, in a little book now forgotten, shown how it was the "basis of all true art, criticism, society, morals, laws, and religion." But of this Society:

First — We may be content to leave almost all, as to what he *undid*, that is matter of discussion at this day whilst partisans define their positions, priests their creeds, with a word which covers it all, *vera pro gratis.* If truth be started, let old errors go.

Next, let us look to what he created and *did.* He ascended to the sublime heights of philosophy and religion ; by thought and study made clear to the intellect the truth that fired his soul, that "God is infinite Perfection, Power, Wisdom, Justice, Love," and plainly showed it to the world. He saw and showed how, historically and by nature, man grows in the light of love and has his eyes opened to spiritual truth, as flowers beneath the sun. He took Truth from books and scholars, Religion from temples and the priests, and showed them to common men.

His basis was *Man's intuition of God and direct perception of His Laws.* We see that the old theologies were most disturbed by his ideas ; as Slavery was, of all institutions, most shaken by his labors. Probably time will show that the most positive and complete of his intellectual works was his Spiritual Theology.

Calmly, and at length, alas with labor too great for that failing frame, thinking death near, — as he said, "up to his shoulders in his grave,"—he reviewed his work. He wished to live to round it off, hoping for the length of years and strength of his ancestors, but ready to pass the golden gates to immortal life. His work is fragmentary in relation to his idea, though so much is in itself complete. He tells us that after his discourse of Matters Pertaining to "Religion," he formed a plan and prepared for the afternoon and evening of his days, to show the "History of the Progressive Development of Religion among the leading Races of Mankind."

What a few in the groves of the academies by the lamp of philosophy, in moments of vision had seen, had become so clear to him that he would not only make it plain and prove it to the reason of men, but would traverse the history of the world and show its growth; show how, by either method, analysis or synthesis, this one truth was the culmination of human thought. Well may we leave theologies, Christologies, creeds, statutes, societies, governments, to take care of themselves.

Success! For fifteen years a free church; this truth embodied in labors for the dangerous, perishing, criminal classes; for education, woman, temperance, freedom, peace; its light thrown on the lives of our great men and heroes; put in volumes that will live with the English tongue; put into labors that now move and will move the American Church and State whilst they endure; set forth in a system of religion; a positive spiritual Theology; a method of spiritual culture; shadowing a scheme of ethics; containing almost the only fit attempt to state the law of Nature, the law of laws, in the language; his thought, his labor, his life —these are success and triumph enough.

After a life brief in years, but in labor how long, in stature how great, in purity how glorious on earth — his mortal robes lie under the skies of Italy. There let them repose, that pilgrims and patriots of the Old World and the New may go to a spot consecrated by blood that flowed thither from English through American veins.

He strove to gird them up for a few years' labor more in the service of God and man, but in vain. The soul that wore them was the world's. It speaks yet, and shall speak in pulpit and senate. Boston will thank him for the unequalled munificence of his charity ; the Herculean labors of his ministry ; the unsullied purity of his life. May she grow to see and live by his truth ; last to have a just pride in being the home of this spiritual Columbus ; forget his errors.

Men may raise monuments of stone ; they will frame memorials more during in adamantine speech. But he who stood here, above the world's fading honors, and his labors will outlast them all.

Our best tribute, — in the presence of the living spirit, the fittest in his sight, and the most lasting, will be the quiet vow not to falter in his work, and, as we may, in church, or court, or state, or common life, to keep in sight the light he showed us and follow its heavenly guidance.

SELECTIONS FROM THE SCRIPTURES,

READ BY JOHN R. MANLEY.

He hath showed thee, O man, what is good, and what doth the Lord require of thee, but to do justly, and to love mercy, and to walk humbly with thy God?

Jesus said unto him, Thou shalt love the Lord thy God with all thy heart, and with all thy soul, and with all thy mind. This is the first and great commandment, and the second is like unto it; Thou shalt love thy neighbor as thyself. On these two commandments hang all the law and the prophets.

But the hour cometh and now is, when the true worshippers shall worship the Father in spirit and in truth, for the Father seeketh such to worship him. God is a spirit, and they who worship him, must worship him in spirit and in truth.

My little children, let us not love in word, neither in tongue; but in deed and in truth. For if our heart condemn us, God is greater than our heart and knoweth all things. Beloved, let us love one another; for love is of God, and every one who loveth is born of God and knoweth God. No man hath seen God at any time. If we love one another, God dwelleth in us, and his love is perfected in us. And we have known and believed the love that God hath to us. God is love, and he who dwelleth in love, dwelleth in God, and God in him. There is no fear in love, but perfect love casteth out all fear, because fear hath torment. He who feareth, is not made perfect in love.

The Lord is my Shepherd, I shall not want. Yea, though I walk through the valley of the shadow of death, I will fear no evil: for thou art with me; thy rod and thy staff they comfort me. Surely goodness and mercy shall follow me all the days of my life; and I will dwell in the house of the Lord forever. When my father and my mother forsake me, then the Lord will take me up. I had fainted, unless I had believed to see the goodness of the Lord in the land of the living.

Then shall the king say unto them on his right hand,
Come, ye blessed of my Father, inherit the kingdom prepared for you from the foundation of the world; For I was
an hungered, and ye gave me meat; I was thirsty, and ye
gave me drink; I was a stranger, and ye took me in; Naked,
and ye clothed me: I was sick, and ye visited me: I was in
prison, and ye came unto me. Then shall the righteous
answer him, saying, Lord, when saw we thee an hungered,
and fed thee? or thirsty, and gave thee drink? When saw
we thee a stranger, and took thee in? or naked, and clothed
thee? Or when saw we thee sick, or in prison, and came
unto thee? And the King shall answer and say unto them,
Verily, I say unto you, inasmuch as ye have done it unto
one of the least of these my brethren, ye have done it unto
me.

Blessed are the poor in spirit; for theirs is the kingdom
of heaven.

Blessed are they who mourn; for they shall be comforted.

Blessed are the meek; for they shall inherit the earth.

Blessed are they which do hunger and thirst after righteousness; for they shall be filled.

Blessed are the merciful, for they shall obtain mercy.

Blessed are the pure in heart; for they shall see God.

Blessed are the peace-makers; for they shall be called the
children of God.

Blessed are they who are persecuted for righteousness'
sake; for theirs is the kingdom of heaven.

Blessed are ye when men shall revile you, and persecute
you, and shall say all manner of evil against you falsely, for
my sake.

Rejoice and be exceeding glad, for great is your reward
in heaven; for so persecuted they the prophets which were
before you.

HYMN 239.

Nearer, my God, to Thee,
  Nearer to Thee!
E'en though it be a cross
  That raiseth me;
Still all my song shall be, —
Nearer, my God, to Thee,
  Nearer to Thee!

Though, like the wanderer,
  The sun gone down,
Darkness be over me,
  My rest a stone;
Yet in my dreams I'd be
Nearer, my God, to Thee, —
  Nearer to Thee!

There let the way appear,
  Steps unto heaven,
All that Thou sendest me,
  In mercy given;
Angels to beckon me
Nearer, my God, to Thee, —
  Nearer to Thee!

Then with my waking thoughts,
  Bright with Thy praise,
Out of my stony griefs,
  Bethel I'll raise:
So by my woes to be
Nearer, my God, to Thee, —
  Nearer to Thee!

Or if on joyful wing,
  Cleaving the sky,
Sun, moon, and stars forgot,
  Upward I fly;
Still all my song shall be, —
Nearer, my God, to Thee,
  Nearer to Thee!

REMARKS BY RALPH WALDO EMERSON.

At the death of a good and admirable person we meet to console and animate each other by the recollection of his virtues. I have the feeling that every man's biography is at his own expense. He furnishes not only the facts but the report. I mean that all biography is autobiography. It is only what he tells of himself that comes to be known and believed. In Plutarch's lives of Alexander and Pericles, you have the secret whispers of their confidence to their lovers and trusty friends. For, it was each report of this kind that impressed those to whom it was told in a manner to secure its being told everywhere to the best, to those who speak with authority to their own times and therefore to ours. For the political rule is a cosmical rule, that if a man is not strong in his own district, he is not a good candidate elsewhere.

He whose voice will not be heard here again, could well afford to tell his experiences; they were all honorable to him, and were part of the history of the civil and religious liberty of his times. Theodore Parker was a son of the soil, charged with the energy of New England, strong, eager, inquisitive of knowledge, of a diligence that never tired, upright, of a haughty independence, yet the gentlest of companions; a man of study, fit for a man of the world; with decided opinions and plenty of power to state them; rapidly pushing his studies so far as to leave few men qualified to sit as his critics. He elected his part of duty, or accepted nobly that assigned him in his rare constitution. Wonderful acquisition of knowledge, a rapid wit that heard all, and welcomed all that came, by seeing its bearing. Such was the largeness of his reception of facts, and his skill to employ them, that it looked as if he were some President of

Council to whom a score of telegraphs were ever bringing in reports; and his information would have been excessive, but for the noble use he made of it, ever in the interest of humanity. He had a strong understanding, a logical method, a love for facts, a rapid eye for their historic relations, and a skill in stripping them of traditional lustres. He had a sprightly fancy, and often amused himself with throwing his meaning into pretty apologues, yet we can hardly ascribe to his mind the poetic element, though his scholarship had made him a reader and quoter of verses. A little more feeling of the poetic significance of his facts, would have disqualified him for some of his severer offices to his generation. The old religions have a charm for most minds which it is a little uncanny to disturb. 'T is sometimes a question, shall we not leave them to decay without rude shocks? I remember that I found some harshness in his treatment both of Greek and of Hebrew antiquity, and sympathized with the pain of many good people in his auditory, whilst I acquitted him, of course, of any wish to be flippant.

He came at a time when to the irresistible march of opinion the forms still retained by the most advanced sects, showed loose and lifeless, and he, with something less of affectionate attachment to the old, or with more vigorous logic, rejected them. 'T is objected to him that he scattered too many illusions. Perhaps more tenderness would have been graceful; but it is vain to charge him with perverting the opinions of the new generation. The opinions of men are organic. Simply, those came to him who found themselves expressed by him. And had they not met this enlightened mind, in which they beheld their own opinions combined with zeal in every cause of love and humanity, they would have suspected their own opinions and suppressed them, and so sunk into melancholy or malignity, a feeling of loneliness and hostility to what was reckoned respectable.

'T is plain to me that he has achieved a historic immortality here; that he has so woven ˈ mself in these few years into the history of Boston, that he can never be left out of your annals. It will not be in the acts of City Councils; nor of obsequious Mayors; nor, in the State House, the proclamations of Governors, with their failing virtue, — failing them at critical moments — that the coming generations will study what really befell; but in the plain lessons of Theodore Parker in this Music Hall, in Faneuil Hall, or in Legislative Committee Rooms, the true temper and authentic record of these days will be read. The next generation will care little for the chances of elections that govern governors now; it will care little for fine gentlemen who behaved shabbily, but it will read very intelligently in his rough story, fortified with exact anecdotes, precise with names and dates, what part was taken by each actor; who threw himself into the cause of humanity, and who came to the rescue of civilization at a hard pinch, and who blocked its course.

The vice charged against America, is the want of sincerity in leading men. It does not lie at his door. He never kept back the truth, for fear to make an enemy. But, on the other hand, it was complained that he was bitter and harsh, that his zeal burned with too hot a flame. It is so difficult, in evil times, to escape this charge! For the faithful preacher most of all. It was his merit, like Luther, Knox, and Latimer, and John Baptist, to speak tart truth, when that was peremptory, and when there were few to say it. But his sympathy for goodness was not less energetic. One fault he had, — he over-estimated his friends, — I may well say it, and sometimes vexed them with the importunity of his good opinion, whilst they knew better the ebb which follows exaggerated praise. He was capable, it must be said, of the most unmeasured eulogies on those he esteemed, especially if he had any jealousy that they did not stand with the Boston public as highly as they ought. His commanding merit as a reformer is this, that he insisted beyond all men in pulpits, — I cannot think of one rival, — that the essence of Christianity is its practical morals ; it is there for use, or it is nothing ; and if you combine it with sharp trading, or with ordinary city ambitions to gloss over municipal corruptions, or private intemperance, or successful fraud, or immoral politics, or unjust wars, or the cheating of Indians, or the robbery of frontier nations, or leaving your principles at home to show on the high seas or in Europe a supple complaisance to tyrants, — it is a hypocrisy, and the truth is not in you ; and no love of religious music or of dreams of Swedenborg, or praise of John Wesley, or of Jeremy Taylor, can save you from the Satan which you are.

His ministry fell on a political crisis also ; on the years when Southern slavery broke over its old banks, made new and vast pretensions, and wrung from the weakness or treachery of Northern people fatal concessions in the Fugitive Slave Bill and the repeal of the Missouri Compromise. Two days, bitter in the memory of Boston, the days of the rendition of Sims and of Burns, made the occasion of his most remarkable discourses. He kept nothing back. In terrible earnest he denounced the public crime, and meted out to every official, high and low, his due portion. By the incessant power of his statement, he made and held a party. It was his great service to freedom. He took away the reproach of silent consent that would otherwise have lain against the indignant minority, by uttering in the hour and place wherein these outrages were done the stern protest.

But whilst I praise this frank speaker, I have no wish to accuse the silence of others. There are men of good powers who have so much sympathy, that they must be silent when they are not in sympathy. If you don't agree with them,

2 *

they know they only injure the truth by speaking. Their faculties will not play them true, and they do not wish to squeak and gibber, and so they shut their mouths. I can readily forgive this, only not the other, the false tongue which makes the worse appear the better cause. There were, of course, multitudes to censure and defame this truth-speaker. But the brave know the brave. Fops, whether in drawing-rooms or churches, will utter the fop's opinion, and faintly hope for the salvation of his soul; but his manly ene-mies, who despised the fops, honored him; and it is well known that his great hospitable heart was the sanctuary to which every soul conscious of an earnest opinion came for sympathy — alike the brave slaveholder and the brave slave-rescuer. These met in the house of this honest man — for every sound heart loves a responsible person, one who does not in generous company say generous things, and in mean company base things, but says one thing, — now cheerfully, now indignantly, — but always because he must, and because he sees, that, whether he speak or refrain from speech, this is said over him; and history, nature, and all souls testify to the same.

Ah, my brave brother! it seems as if, in a frivolous age, our loss were immense, and your place cannot be supplied. But you will already be consoled in the transfer of your genius, knowing well that the nature of the world will affirm to all men, in all times, that which for twenty-five years you valiantly spoke; that the winds of Italy murmur the same truth over your grave; the winds of America over these bereaved streets; that the sea which bore your mourners home affirms it, the stars in their courses, and the inspira-tions of youth; whilst the polished and pleasant traitors to human rights, with perverted learning and disgraced graces, rot and are forgotten with their double tongue saying all that is sordid for the corruption of man.

The sudden and singular eminence of Mr. Parker, the importance of his name and influence, are the verdict of his country to his virtues. We have few such men to lose; amiable and blameless at home, feared abroad as the standard-bearer of liberty, taking all the duties he could grasp, and more, refusing to spare himself, he has gone down in early glory to his grave, to be a living and enlarging power, wherever learning, wit, honest valor, and independence are honored.

ORIGINAL ODE.

BY FRANKLIN B. SANBORN.

FAIR summer glides with face serene,
  Along the quickening earth to-day;
In murmuring woods and pastures green
  The thrush and sparrow carol gay.

But ours must be the song of wo,
  And tears and wintry gloom are ours,
For one brave heart that lies below
  The tender grass and laughing flowers.

Across the melancholy wave
  Our constant thought flies swiftly there,
And lingers hovering round his grave,
  Amid the fragrant Tuscan air.

O, rest in peace! from labors rest!
  Too long thy blest release we weep;
Thy body sleeps in Earth's kind breast,
  Its loftier way thy soul doth keep.

With us, with us thy memory dwells,
  Forbids despair, and hushes strife, —
Here most, where every echo tells
  The story of thy noble life.

Yet what can check our sorrow here?
Or who more justly weep than we,
While Love and Reverence force the tear,
And Truth and Freedom mourn for thee?

REMARKS BY WENDELL PHILLIPS.

The lesson of this desk is Truth! That your brave teacher dared to speak, and no more. It is only two or three times in our lives that we pause in telling the whole merit of a friend, from fear of being thought flatterers. What the world thinks easily done, it believes; all beyond is put down to fiction. I find myself hesitating to speak just all I think of THEODORE PARKER, lest those who did not know him should suppose I flatter, and thus I mar the massive simplicity of his fame.

Born on the 24th of August, 1810, he died just before finishing his fiftieth year. He said to me, years ago, "When I am fifty, I will leave the pulpit, and finish the great works I have planned." God ordered it so! He has left this desk, and gone there to finish the great works that he planned! Some speak of his death as early; but he died in good old age, if we judge him by his work, — full of labors, if not of years, — a long life crowded into few years; as Bacon says, "Old in hours, for he lost no time." Truly, he lost not an hour, from the early years when, in his sweet, plain phrase, he tells us "his father let the baby pick up chips, drive the cows to pasture, and carry *nubs* of corn to the oxen" — far on to the closing moment when, faint and dying, he sent us his blessing and brave counsel last November, dated fitly from ROME. God granted him life long enough to see of the labor of his hands. He planted broadly, and lived to gather a rich, ripe harvest. His life, too, was an harmonious whole, —

—— "when brought
Among the tasks of real life, he wrought,
Upon the plan that pleased his childish thought."

The very last page those busy fingers ever wrote, tells the child's story, than which, he says, "no event in my life has made so deep and lasting an impression on me." "A little boy in petticoats, in my fourth year, my father sent me from the field home." A spotted tortoise, in shallow water, at the foot of a rhodora, caught his sight, and he lifted his stick to strike it, when "a voice within said, 'it is wrong.' I stood with lifted stick, in wonder at the new emotion, till rhodora and tortoise vanished from my sight. I hastened home, and asked my mother what it was that told me it was wrong. Wiping a tear with her apron, and taking me in her arms, she said, 'Some men call it conscience; but I prefer to call it the voice of God in the soul of man. If you listen to it and obey it, then it will speak clearer and clearer, and always guide you right. But if you turn a deaf ear or disobey, then it will fade out, little by little, and leave you in the dark and without a guide.'"

Out of that tearful mother's arms grew your pulpit. Here in words — every day in the streets, by deeds, during a hard life, he repeated and obeyed her counsel.

Of that pulpit, its theology, and its treatment by Unitarian divines, manly and Christian lips spoke to us two weeks ago. It is not for me, even if there were need, to touch on it. Born in that faith, and nurtured in similar maxims of the utmost liberty, and the duty of individual investigation and thought, I used it to enter other paths. Mine is the old faith of New England. On those points he and I rarely talked. What he thought, I hardly know. For myself, standing beneath the Gospel rule of "judging men by their fruits," I should have felt stronger in defending my own

faith, could I have pointed to any preacher of it who as
gently judged and as truly loved his fellow men. As to
doctrines, we both knew that "the whole of truth can never
do harm to the whole of virtue;" that, of course, a man's
conception of truth is only his opinion, and not, necessarily,
absolute truth. But it is always safe and wise for honest
and earnest men to seek for truth everywhere and at all
hazards. The results, if not wholly and only good, are yet
the best things within our reach.

The lesson of Theodore Parker's preaching was love.
Let me read for you a sonnet still among his papers :

> Oh, Brother! who for us didst meekly wear
>   The Crown of Thorns about thy radiant brow ;
> What Gospel from the Father didst thou bear,
>   Our hearts to cheer, making us happy now ?
> 'Tis this alone, the immortal Saviour cries,
>   To fill thy heart with ever-active love ;
> Love for the wicked as in sin he lies,
>   Love for thy Brother here, thy God above ;
> Fear nothing ill, 't will finish in its day,
>   Live for the Good, taking the ill thou must ;
> Toil with thy might, with manly labor pray,
>   Living and loving learn thy God to trust,
> And He will shed upon thy soul the blessings of the just.

Standing in the old ways, I cannot but suspect these Unitarian pulpits of some latent and cowardly distrust of their own
creed, when I see that if one comes from them to our Orthodox ranks, and believes a great deal more than they do,
he is treated with reverend respect ; but let him go out on
the other side, and believe a very little less, and the whole
startled body join in begging the world not to think them
naturally the parents of such horrible and dangerous
heresy !

But there is one thing every man may say of this pulpit.

It was a live reality, and no sham. Whether tearing theological idols to pieces at West Roxbury, or here, battling with the every-day evils of the streets, it was ever a live voice, and no mechanical or parrot tune: ever fresh from the heart of God, as these flowers, these lilies — the last flower over which, when eyesight failed him, with his old gesture, he passed his loving hand and said, "how sweet!" As in that story he loved so much to tell, of Michael Angelo, when in the Roman palace Raphael was drawing his figures too small, Angelo sketched a colossal head of fit proportions, and taught Raphael his fault, — so Parker criticized these other pulpits, not so much by censure as by creation; by a pulpit proportioned to the hour, broad as humanity, frank as truth, stern as justice, and loving as Christ.

Here is the place to judge him. In St. Paul's Cathedral, the epitaph says, if you would know the genius of Christopher Wren, "look around." Do you ask proof how full were the hands, how large the heart, how many-sided the brain of your teacher — listen, and you will hear it in the glad, triumphant certainty of your enemies, that you must close these doors since his place can never be filled! Do you ask proof of his efficient labor and the good soil into which that seed fell — gladden your eyes by looking back and seeing for how many months the impulse his vigorous hand gave you has sufficed, spite of boding prophecy, to keep these doors open! Yes, he has left those accustomed to use weapons, and not merely to hold up *his* hands. And not only among yourselves. From another city, I received a letter, full of deep feeling, and the writer, an orthodox church-member, says —

"I was a convert to Theodore Parker before I was a convert to ——. If there is any thing of value in the work I am doing to-day, it may, in an important sense, be said to have had its root in Parker's heresy. I mean the habit, without which orthodoxy stands emasculated and good for nothing, of independently passing on the empty and rotten pretensions of churches and churchmen, which I learned earliest and more than from any other from Theodore Parker. He has my love, my respect, my admiration."

Yes, his diocese is broader than Massachusetts. His influence extends very far outside these walls. Every pulpit in Boston is freer and more real to-day because of the existence of this. The fan of his example scattered the chaff of a hundred sapless years. Our whole city is fresher to-day because of him. The most sickly and timid soul under yonder steeple, hide-bound in days and forms and beggarly Jewish elements, little dreams how ten times worse and narrower it was before this sun warmed the general atmosphere around. As was said of Burke's unsuccessful impeachment of Warren Hastings, "never was the great object of punishment, the prevention of crime, more completely obtained. Hastings was acquitted, but *tyranny and injustice were condemned* wherever English was spoken." So we may say of Boston and Theodore Parker. Grant that few adopted his extreme theological views — that not many sympathized in his politics; still, that Boston is nobler, purer, braver, more loving, more Christian to-day, is due more to him than to all the pulpits that vex her Sabbath air. He raised the level of sermons intellectually and morally. Other preachers were compelled to grow in manly thought and Christian morals in very self-defence. The droning routine of dead metaphysics or dainty morals was gone. As Christ preached of the fall of the tower of Siloam the week before, and what men said of it in the streets of Jerusalem, so Parker rung through our startled city the news of some fresh crime against humanity — some slave hunt, or wicked court, or prostituted official — till frightened audiences actually took bond of their new clergymen that they should not be tormented before their time!

Men say he erred on that great question of our age — the place due to the Bible. Perhaps so. But William Crafts, one of the bravest men who ever fled from our vulture to Victoria, writes to a friend : " When the slave-hunters were on our track, and no other minister, except yourself, came to direct our attention to the God or the oppressed, Mr. Parker came with his wise counsel, and told us where and how to go ; gave us money — but that was not all — he gave me a weapon to protect our liberties, and a Bible to guide our souls. I have that Bible now, and shall ever prize it most highly."

How direct and frank his style — just level to the nation's ear. No man ever needed to read any one of his sentences twice to catch its meaning. None suspected that he thought other than he said, or more than he confessed.

Like all such men, he grew daily — never too old to learn. Mark how closer to actual life, how much bolder in reform, are all his later sermons — especially since he came to the city — every year a step

  ——" forward, persevering to the last,
From well to better, daily self-surpassed."

There are men whom we measure by their times — content and expecting to find them subdued to what they work in. They are the chameleons of circumstance; they are Eolian harps, toned by the breeze that sweeps over them. There are others, who serve as guide-posts and land-marks — we measure their times by them. Such was Theodore Parker. Hereafter the critic will use him as a mete-wand, to measure the heart and civilization of Boston. Like the Englishman, a year or two ago, who suspected our great historian could not move in the best circles of the city, when it dropped out that he did not know Theodore Parker, distant men gauge us by our toleration and recognition of him.

Such men are our Nilometers; the harvest of thé future is according to the height that the flood of our love rises round them. Who cares now that Harvard vouchsafed him no honors! But history will save the fact to measure the calculating and prudent bigotry of our times.

Some speak of him only as a bitter critic and harsh prophet. Pulpits and journals shelter their plain speech in mentioning him under the example of what they call his "unsparing candor." Do they feel that the *strangeness* of their speech, their unusual frankness, needs apology and example! But he was far other than a bitter critic; though thank God for every drop of that bitterness that came like a wholesome rebuke on the dead, saltless sea of American life! Thank God for every indignant protest, for every Christian admonition that the Holy Spirit breathed through those manly lips! But if he deserved any single word, it was "generous." *Vir generosus* is the description that leaps to the lip of every scholar. He was generous of money. Born on a New England farm, in those days when small incomings made every dollar a matter of importance, he no sooner had command of wealth than he lived with open hands. Not even the darling ambition of a great library ever tempted him to close his ear to need. Go to Venice or Vienna, to Frankfort or to Paris, and ask the refugees who have gone back, — when here friendless exiles but for him, — under whose roof they felt most at home! One of our oldest and best teachers writes me, that telling him once, in the cars, of a young lad of rare mathematical genius, who could read Laplace, but whom narrow means debarred from the University — "Let him enter," said Theodore Parker; "I will pay his bills."

No sect, no special study, no one idea bounded his sympathy; but he was generous in judgment, where a common man would have found it hard to be so. Though he does not "go down to dust without his fame," though Oxford and Germany sent him messages of sympathy, still, no word of approbation from the old grand names of our land, no honors from University or learned Academy, greeted his brave, diligent, earnest life ; men can confess that they voted against his admission to ..cientific bodies for his ideas, feeling all the while that his brain could furnish half the Academy ; and yet, thus ostracized, he was the most generous, more than just, interpreter of the motives of those about him, and looked on while others reaped where he sowed, with most generous joy in their success. Patiently analyzing character and masterly in marshalling facts, he stamped with generous justice the world's final judgment of Webster, and now that the soreness of the battle is over, friend and foe allow it.

He was generous of labor, — books never served to excuse him from any, — the humblest work. Though "hiving wisdom with each studious year," and passionately devoted to his desk, as truly as was said of Milton, " The lowliest duties on himself he laid." What drudgery of the street did that scholarly hand ever refuse ? Who so often and constant as he in the trenches, when a slave case made our city a camp ? Loving books, he had no jot of a scholar's indolence or timidity, but joined hands with labor everywhere. Erasmus would have found him good company, and Melanchthon got brave help over a Greek manuscript ; but the likeliest place to have found him in that age would have been at Zwingle's side, on the battle-field, pierced with a score of fanatic spears. For, above all things, he was terribly in earnest. If I sought to paint him in one word, I should say he was always *in earnest.*

I spoke once of his diligence, and we call him tireless, unflagging, unresting. But they are common-place words, and poorly describe him. What we usually call diligence in educated men does not outdo, does not equal the day-laborer in ceaselessness of toil. No scholar, not even the busiest, but loiters out from his weary books, and feels shamed by the hodman or the plough-boy. The society and amusements of easy life eat up and beguile one half our time. Those on whose lips and motions hang crowds of busy idlers, submit to life-long discipline, almost every hour a lesson. Those on whose tones float the most precious truth, disdain an effort. The table you write on is the fruit of more toilsome and thorough discipline than the brain of most who deem themselves scholars ever knew. Let us not cheat ourselves with words. But no poor and greedy mechanic, no farm tenant " on shares " ever distanced this unresting brain. He brought into his study that conscientious, loving industry which six generations had handed down to him on the hard soil of Massachusetts. He *loved* work, and I doubt if any workman in our empire equalled him in thoroughness of preparation. Before he wrote his review of Prescott, he went conscientiously through all the printed histories of that period in three or four tongues. Before he ventured to paint for you the portrait of John Quincy Adams, he read every line Adams ever printed, and all the attacks upon him that could be found in public or private collections.

Fortunate man! he lived long enough to see the eyes of the whole nation turned toward him as to a trusted teacher. Fortunate, indeed, in a life so noble, that even what was scorned from the pulpit, will surely become oracular from the tomb! Thrice fortunate, if he loved fame and future influence, that the leaves which bear his thoughts to posterity are not freighted with words penned by sickly ambition or wrung from hunger, — but with earnest thoughts on dangers that make the ground tremble under our feet, and the heaven black over our head, — the only literature sure to live. Ambition says, " I will write, and be famous." It is only a dainty tournament, a sham fight, forgotten when the smoke clears away. Real books are like Yorktown or Waterloo, whose cannon shook continents at the moment, and echo down the centuries. Through such channels Parker poured his thoughts.

And true hearts leaped to his side. No man's brain ever made him warmer friends ; no man's heart ever held them firmer. He loved to speak of how many hands he had, in every city, in every land, ready to work for him. With royal serenity he levied on all. Vassal hearts multiplied the great chief's powers. And at home the gentlest and deepest love, saintly, unequalled devotion, made every hour sunny, held off every care, and left him double liberty to work. God comfort that widowed heart !

Judge him by his friends. No man suffered anywhere, who did not feel sure of his sympathy. In sick chambers, and by the side of suffering humanity, he kept his heart soft and young. No man lifted a hand anywhere for truth and right, who did not look on Theodore Parker as his fellow-laborer. When men hoped for the future, this desk was one stone on which they planted their feet. Where, more frequent than around his board, would you find men familiar with Europe's dungeons and the mobs of our own streets ? Wherever the fugitive slave might worship, here was his Gibraltar. Over his mantel, however scantily furnished, in this city or elsewhere, you were sure to find a picture of Parker.

But he is gone ! So certain was he of his death, that in the still watches of the Italian night, he comforted the sickening hopes of those about him by whispering —

> " I hear a voice you cannot hear,
> Which says I must not stay ;
> I see a hand you cannot see,
> Which beckons me away."

3 *

But where shall we stop? This empty desk! You may fill it, but where is he who called it into being? Who shall make it so emphatically the symbol of free thought? To have stood here was, for most men, sufficient credentials. Here the young knight earned his spurs. Around it has swelled and tossed the battle of Christian liberty. The debate, whether Theodore Parker should speak in one place or preach in another, has been one of God's chief methods of teaching this land the lesson of what bigots style *toleration*, and freemen better call Christian liberty.

He has passed on — we linger. That other world grows more real to us, as friend after friend enters it. Soon more are there than on this side; soon our hearts are more than half there. God tenderly sunders the few ties that still bind us. So live that when called to join that other assembly, we shall feel we are only passing from an apprenticeship of thought and toil to broader fields and a higher teacher above.

The blessings of the poor are his laurels. Say that his words won doubt and murmur to trust in a loving God — let that be his record! Say that to the hated and friendless, he was shield and buckler — let that be his epitaph! The glory of children is the fathers. When you voted " that Theodore Parker should be heard in Boston," God honored you. Well have you kept that pledge. In much labor and with many sacrifices he has laid the corner-stone. His work is ended here. God calls you to put on the top-stone. Let fearless lips and Christian lives be his monument!

HYMN 327.

My God, I thank Thee! may no thought
E'er deem Thy chastisements severe;
But may this heart, by sorrow taught,
Calm each wild wish, each idle fear.

Thy mercy bids all nature bloom ;
   The sun shines bright, and man is gay ;
Thine equal mercy spreads the gloom
   That darkens o'er his little day.

Full many a throb of grief and pain
   Thy frail and erring child must know ;
But not one prayer is breathed in vain,
   Nor does one tear unheeded flow.

Thy various messengers employ ;
   Thy purposes of love fulfil ;
And 'mid the wreck of human joy,
   Let kneeling faith adore Thy will.

The exercises were concluded with a benediction pronounced by Rev. Mr. Russell.

The following letter was received from Mr. Wasson, and would have been read had not the length of the exercises prevented : —

LETTER FROM D. A. WASSON.

Not only ages, but entire civilizations may pass, before another man shall arise, just so gifted and equipped as him whom we commemorate to-day. It is not so much that his powers were rare in kind, though they were surely rare — very rare in degree; but his distinction is that he combined in himself qualities, which commonly go to the making of a large number of men, and are considered incompatible ; and, as oxygen and carbon in their chemical union make flame, and hydrogen and oxygen produce water, though in their separate accumulation the former are cold and the latter dry, so qualities and powers which separately would have made only a multitude of strong men, in their vital union produced that brand of the Lord, that Missouri of manhood, whom we remember as Theodore Parker. Winckelmann, in his work on Greek art, shows that the finest forms were achieved by an admirable blending into one of the characteristics of man and woman; and I think that in great excellence everywhere there is a conjunction of natural opposites. So was it with our hero. He was in spirit a union of Cato the Censor, and some sweetest Sister of Charity; he was both Freya, the gentle and prophetic, and Thor with the thunder hammer. So while his learning and reading were so vast that the entire faculty of a college could have been well fitted out from his single brain, on the other hand, he could teach common sense to mechanics, homely simplicity of speech to draymen, and sympathy with the every-day interests of mankind to all. He was more a recluse student than any merest scholar; and he inhabited a wider out-of-doors than sea-captains. He had such trust in God and such sureness of the future, — or rather a thousand times more than such — as those have who " wait God's time ; " while yet he toiled as though the weight of the world rested upon his shoulders alone, and as if no plant of blessing should spring up for the future whose seed was not sown out of his own heart. It is often said that he was chiefly a destroyer. That is not true. He joined opposites here as elsewhere. He indeed pulled down with power, but also with power and assiduity he built up. He spurned the false ; but it was for love of the true. He lopped away with an unsparing hand the foolish or hidden excrescences of theological speculation ; but so much and more did he enlarge and affirm the simple elements, the universal truths, of faith and morals. But I misstate — I said that he pulled down ; — this, however, is not so. To cleanse the Augean stables is not to destroy them. To push away ruin and corruption is no work of destruction. He *swept*, indeed, the house of Faith, intolerant of the abominations which profaned it ; but at the same time, and with no less industrious hand, he strengthened and buttressed its walls. He was a reverent man, — profoundly religious and reverent. True, he did not split hairs about the Trinity ; he did not maunder of the Logos ; he did not prate of the Fathers ; he was not tender toward superstitions that slander God ; and did not earn a cheap reputation for a reverent habit so ; but that man is reverent who bows before the attributes of God, and who can honor all men, be they white or black ; that man is reverent to whom justice is commanding and goodness adorable ; and of whom could this be affirmed more than of Theodore Parker ?

He was a rare learner, humble, docile, intent; a perpetual child at the text-book of Nature, constantly correcting himself, never ashamed to confess a mistake ; yet he had preeminently the spirit and genius of a teacher, — methodical, clear, positive, endlessly varying his statements, and never, by a hundred or a thousand repetitions of his cardinal facts and doctrines, wearying either himself or his hearers.

So self-respecting he was that he forgot not the rights of his manhood even in the most awed moment of his adoration — so humble that there was no hind, no idiot, to whom his heart beat not with equal love as a brother. He was capable of a mighty wrath, but it was born of his love, and never expended upon account of his private wrongs; he was angry and sinned not, for it was the anger of the prophet ; indignation at wrongs done to humanity ; a grand, a noble, a sacred passion. Treachery to truth, to justice, to mercy, to God and man — this it was, and this alone, that flushed his brow. A blow at himself he never in his life returned ; but the wretch, especially the great, the powerful, the prosperous wretch, who came to stab at the heart of humanity, him he confronted, and in no trivial mood ! He was the war-horse of God — he was the Cœur de Lion of conscience and common sense — he was a sanctified Titan — he was THEODORE PARKER !

PROCEEDINGS

OF

THE NEW ENGLAND ANTI-SLAVERY CONVENTION.

AT the session of the New England Anti-Slavery Convention, on Thursday afternoon, May 31, the following Resolutions were offered by Wendell Phillips:—

Resolved, That in the death of our beloved friend and fellow-laborer, Theodore Parker, liberty, justice, and truth lose one of their ablest and foremost champions — one whose tireless industry, whose learning, the broadest, most thorough and profound New England knows, whose masterly intellect, melted into a brave and fervent heart, earned for him the widest and most abiding influence; in the service of truth and right, lavish of means, prodigal of labor, fearless in utterance; the most Christian minister at God's altar in all our Commonwealth, one of the few whose fidelity saves the name of the ministry from being justly a reproach and byword with religious and thinking men; a kind, true heart, full of womanly tenderness—the object of the most unscrupulous even of bigot and priestly hate, yet on whose garments bitter and watchful malice found no stain — laying on the altar the fruits of the most unresting toil, yet ever ready as the idlest to man any post of daily and humble duty at any moment:—in him we lose that strong sense, deep feeling and love of right for whose eloquent voice millions waited in every hour of darkness and peril, whose last word came, fitly, across the water a salutation and a blessing to the kindred martyrs of Harper's Ferry :— the store-house of the lore of every language and age, the armory of a score of weapons sacred to right, the leader whose voice was the bond of a mighty host, the friend ever sincere, loyal, and vigilant, a man whose fidelity was attested equally by the trust of those who loved him, and the hate of every thing selfish, heartless, and base in the land; in time to come the slave will miss keenly that voice always heard in his behalf, and which a nation was learning to heed—and whoever anywhere lifts a hand for any victim of wrong and sin, will be lonelier and weaker for the death we mourn to-day.

Resolved, That a copy of the above resolution be sent to Mrs. Parker, with fit expression of our most sincere and respectful sympathy in this hour of her bitter grief and sad bereavement.

REMARKS BY REV. JOHN T. SARGENT,

PRESIDENT OF THE CONVENTION.

I can only say, for myself, that, perhaps, I have no right to a single moment of the precious time, so wisely assigned to other speakers ; but this let me say, as the presiding officer of this Convention, that under no auspices, perhaps, could this fitting tribute be more suitably and profitably offered, than under those of the New England Anti-Slavery Convention ; and, were the tribute to be commensurate with the worth of our dear friend, it might better be said, under the auspices of the United States Anti-Slavery Convention, or the wide world's Anti-Slavery Convention. For who more than he has been the fearless champion of human rights?

This, as was said yesterday, of all places in this city of his professional labors, is the fitting place for our tribute; for you remember it was here that he first planted the standard of freedom of speech and the freedom of the pulpit, which he so manfully and nobly sustained to the hour of his death. I am sure there are many here present who well remember the stormy day, the memorable sixteenth of February, 1845, when we met here his few and fondly-attached followers, and here inaugurated that freedom which he so bravely carried out.

But, as I said when I began, I have no right — though my heart is full enough, Heaven knows — to encroach upon the time which has been assigned to other and abler speakers. You are to hear, this afternoon, from Wendell Phillips, and others who knew and loved our friend — the friend of man.

REMARKS BY REV. SAMUEL J. MAY.

Mr. President : — I shall not detain you or the Convention long with what I have to say. You are all expecting, and expecting justly, from the lips of him who has just read to you the resolutions, a speech which will be more worthy of them and of the occasion than any thing that I can offer. But I deem it a privilege as well as a duty first to press upon you — if, indeed, they need to be pressed — those resolutions, expressive of the sorrow which every one who had aught to do with this or any other attempted reforms in our country must feel, when they think of the departure of those who have been so true, so faithful, so fearless. I look back, Mr. President, with a sad heart upon the past, when I remember not only these two faithful ones, but others who have fallen, ere yet the great work to which we put our hands, a few years ago, seems to be half accomplished. When I first heard our brother Garrison state and advocate the great principles on which the redemption of the enslaved in our country was to be attempted, they seemed to me so self-evidently true, they were so impressive, that I had not a doubt of their almost immediate acceptance when they should be made known. So simple was I in that day of Anti-Slavery infancy! In 1840, a dear friend, my step-mother, died. She had ever, however, I am sorry to say, been opposed to my espousal of the Anti-Slavery cause; for though excellent in other respects, she was constitutionally conservative. I refer to her now, that I may mention a fact which I had forgotten for some time. Among her papers was one dated about ten years before the time when I found it, on which was recorded this simple prediction of mine:— "Our son, S. J. May, says that, in ten years from this time, the Anti-Slavery cause must be triumphant." That was in 1840. How little did I foresee the trials to which this self-evident truth was to be subjected, ere it would be accepted by the people! Never shall I forget the joy of my heart when our friends, Phillips and Quincy, came forth, with all their academic honors upon them, and all their professional prospects before them, and laid themselves, and all they were and had, upon the altar of devotion to the slave. It seemed to me the harbinger of almost immediate triumph to our cause. But we toiled on, year after year, and still the mighty Bastile stood, apparently as firm as ever. Then came the men who are alluded to in these resolutions. And more especially Theodore Parker, of whom all that is here set forth may be said, and more, if language could be found to express it. A truer, purer, simpler, more devout, devoted, fearless, loving man, have I never known. And yet, what have his labors, and all the labors of brother Browne, and of all who have come into this cause, effected? The nation is indeed aroused; the nation can never slumber again over this mighty wrong;—that is true. The day of triumph must come, for there is a God, and there is a spark of Divinity in every human heart, else man would not be man. And yet, who is confident enough to prophesy when the hour is to be? But let us not be discouraged. In grateful memory of these devoted friends, in grateful memory of the services rendered us by that man, especially, whose memory is to live, and whose fame is to spread wider and wider, and whose loving and burning words are to be listened to by an ever enlarging audience throughout every part of those lands which speak our language — aye, and all other lands in which there is any thing like free thought — in grateful remembrance of his services, and as the best testimony we can give him of our gratitude and love, let us now, with renewed devotion, consecrate ourselves all the more to this great service, in the solemn resolution that, crippled as we are by his removal from our midst, yet, trusting in that God whom he so nobly vindicated from the aspersions that a false theology has thrown upon him, and to the power of that truth which possesses, in itself, an influence which the stoutest, the most malignant, cannot forever withstand — let us, I say, resolve that, crippled as we are, we will nevertheless go on with increased determination, fighting this monster-wrong to its death.

REMARKS BY WENDELL PHILLIPS.

Another friend is gone. Not gone! No, with us, only standing on one step higher than he did. To such spirits, there is no death. In the old times, when men fought with spears, the warrior hurled his weapon into the thickest of the opposite host, and struggled bravely on, until he stood over it and reclaimed it. In the bloom of his youth, Theodore Parker flung his heart forward at the feet of the Eternal;

he has only struggled onward, and reached it to-day. Only one step higher!

> "Wail ye may full well for Scotland,
> Let none dare to mourn for him."

How shall we group his qualities? The first that occurs to me is the tireless industry of that unresting brain, which never seemed to need leisure. When some engagement brought me home in the small hours of the morning, many and many a time have I looked out (my own window commands those of his study), and seen that unquenched light burning — that unflagging student ever at work. Half curious, half ashamed, I lay down, saying with the Athenian, "The trophies of Miltiades will not let me sleep." He seemed to rebuke me even by the light that flashed from the window of his study. I have met him on the cars deep in some strange tongue, or hiving up knowledge to protect the weak and hated of his own city. Neither on the journey nor at home did his spirit need to rest.

Why is he dead? Because he took up the burden of three men. A faithful pulpit is enough for one man. He filled it until the fulness of his ideas overflowed into other channels. It was not enough. His diocese extended to the prairies. On every night of the week, those brave lips smothered bigotry, conquered prejudice, and melted true hearts into his own on the banks of the Mississippi. This was enough for two men. But he said, "I will bring to this altar of Reform a costlier offering yet;" and he gathered the sheaf of all literature into his bosom, and came with another man's work, almost all the thoughts of all ages and all tongues, as the background of his influence in behalf of the slave. He said, "Let no superficial scholarship presume to arraign Reform as arrogant and empty fanaticism. I will overtop your candidates with language and law, and show you, in all tongues, by argument̄s hoar with antiquity, the rightfulness and inevitable necessity of justice and liberty." Enough work for three men to do; and he sunk under the burden.

Lord Bacon says, " Studies teach not their own use; that comes from a wisdom without them and above them." The fault of New England scholarship is that it knows not its own use; that, as Bacon says, " it settles in its fixed wayˢ, and does not seek reformation." The praise of this scholar is, that, like the great master of English philosophy, he was content to light his torch at every man's candle. He was not ashamed to learn. When he started in the pulpit, he came a Unitarian, with the blessings of Cambridge. Men say he is a Unitarian no longer; but the manna, when it was kept two days, bred maggots, and the little worms that run about on the surface of corruption call themselves the children and representatives of Channing. They are only the worms of the manna, and the pulpit of Federal Street found its child at the Music Hall. God's lineage is not of blood. Brewster of Plymouth, if he stood here to-day, would not be in the Orthodox Church, counting on his anxious fingers the five points of Calvin. No; he would be shouldering a Sharpe's rifle in Kansas; fighting against the libels of the *Independent* and *Observer ;* preaching treason in Virginia, and hung on an American gibbet; — for the child of Puritanism is not mere Calvinism; it is the loyalty to justice which tramples under foot the wicked laws of its own epoch. So Unitarianism (so far as it has any worth) is not standing in the same pulpit, or muttering the same shibboleth; it is, like Channing, looking into the face of a national sin, and, with lips touched like Isaiah's, finding it impossible not to launch at it the thunderbolt of God's rebuke.

Old Lyman Beecher said, " If you want to find the successor of St. Paul, seek him where you find the same objec-

tions made to a preacher that were made to St. Paul."
Who won the hatred of the merchant princes of Boston?
Who did State street call a madman? The fanatic of Federal street in 1837. Who, with unerring instinct, did that
same herd of merchant princes hate, with instinctive certainty that, in order that their craft should be safe, they
ought to hate him? The Apostle of Music Hall. That is
enough.

When some Americans die — when most Americans die
— their friends tire the public with excuses. They confess
this spot, they explain that stain, they plead circumstances
as the half justification of that mistake, and they beg of us to
remember that nothing but good is to be spoken of the dead.
We need no such mantle for that green grave under the sky
of Florence. No excuses — no explanations — no spot.
Priestly malice has scanned every inch of his garment; — it
was seamless; it could find no stain. History, as in the case
of every other of her beloved children, gathers into her
bosom the arrows which malice had shot at him, and says to
posterity, "Behold the title-deeds of your gratitude!" We
ask no moment to excuse, there is nothing to explain. What
the snarling journal thought bold, what the selfish politician
feared as his ruin — it was God's seal set upon his apostleship.
The little libel glanced across him like a rocket when it goes
over the vault; it is passed, and the royal sun shines out as
beneficent as ever.

When I returned from New York on the thirteenth day
of this month, I was to have been honored by standing in
his desk, but illness prevented my fulfilling the appointment.
It was eleven o'clock in the morning. As he sank away
the same week, under the fair sky of Italy, he said to the
most loving of wives and of nurses, "Let me be buried
where I fall;" and tenderly, thoughtfully, she selected four

o'clock of the same Sunday to mingle his dust with the kindred dust of brave, classic Italy.

Four o'clock! The same sun that looked upon the half-dozen mourners that he permitted to follow him to the grave, that same moment of brightness lighted up the arches of his own Temple, as one whom he loved stepped into his own desk, and with remarkable coincidence, for the only time during his absence, opened one of his own sermons to supply my place; and as his friend read the Beatitudes over his grave on the banks of the Arno, his dearer friend here read from a manuscript the text, "Have faith in God." It is said that, in his last hours, in the wandering of that masterly brain, he murmured, "There are two Theodore Parkers; one rests here, dying, but the other lives, and is at work at home." How true! at that very moment, he was speaking to his usual thousands; at that very instant, his own words were sinking down into the hearts of those that loved him best, and bidding them, in this, the loneliest hour of their bereavement, "Have faith in God."

He always came to this platform. He is an old occupant of it. He never made an apology for coming to it. I remember many years ago, going home from the very hall which formerly occupied this place. He had sat where you sit, in the seats, looking up to us. It had been a stormy, hard gathering — a close fight; the press calumniating us; every journal in Boston ridiculing the idea which we were endeavoring to spread. As I passed down the stairs homeward, he put his arm within mine, and said, "You shall never need to ask me again to share that platform." It was the instinct of his nature, true as the bravest heart. The spot for him was where the battle was hottest. He had come, as half the clergy come — a critic. He felt it was not his place; that it was to grapple with the tiger, and throttle him. And the pledge that he made he kept; for, whether here or in New York, as his reputation grew, when that lordly mammoth of the press, the *Tribune*, overgrown in its independence and strength, would not condescend to record a word that Mr. Garrison or I could utter, but bent low before the most thorough scholarship of New England, and was glad to win its way to the confidence of the West by being his mouthpiece — with that weapon of influence in his right hand, he always placed himself at our side, and in the midst of us, in the capital State of the Empire.

You may not think this great praise — we do. Other men have brought us brave hearts, other men have brought us keen-sighted and vigilant intellects, but he brought us, as no one else could, the loftiest stature of New England culture. He brought us a disciplined intellect, whose statement was evidence, and whose affirmation the most gifted student took long time before he ventured to doubt or to contradict. When we had nothing but our characters, nothing but our reputation for accuracy, for our weapons, the man who could give to the cause of the slave that weapon, was indeed one of its ablest and foremost champions.

Lord Bacon said in his will, "I leave my name and memory to foreign lands, and to my own countrymen, *after some time be passed*." No more fitting words could be chosen, if the modesty of the friend who has just gone before us would have permitted him to adopt them for himself. To-day, even within twenty-four hours, I have seen symptoms of that repentance which Johnson describes:

> "When nations, slowly wise and meanly just,
> To buried merit raise the tardy bust."

The men who held their garments aside, and desired to have no contact with Music Hall, are beginning to show symptoms that they will be glad, when the world doubts whether they have any life left, to say, "Did not Theodore Parker spring from our bosom?" Yes, he takes his place — his serene place — among those few to whom Americans point as a proof that the national heart is still healthy and alive. Most of our statesmen, most of our politicians, go down into their graves, and we cover them up with apologies; we walk with reverent and filial love backward, and throw the mantle over their defects, and say, "Remember the temptation and the time!" Now and then one — now and then one — goes up silently, and yet not unannounced, like the stars at their coming, and takes its place, while all eyes follow it and say, "Thank God! It is the promise and the herald! It is the nation alive at its heart. God has not left us without a witness, for his children have been among us, and one half have known them by love, and one half have known them by hate — equal attestations to the divine life that has passed through our streets."

I wish I could say any thing worthy; but he should have done for us, with the words that never failed to be fitting, with that heart which was always ready, with that eloquence which you never waited for and were disappointed — he should have done for us what we vainly try to do for him. Farewell, brave, strong friend and helper!

> "Sleep in peace with kindred ashes
> Of the noble and the true;
> Hands that never failed their country,
> Hearts that baseness never knew!"

REMARKS BY WM. LLOYD GARRISON.

Mr. Garrison said he felt impelled to utter a few unpremeditated words in support of the resolutions offered by

Mr. Phillips, respecting the removal of his beloved and en-
deared friend, THEODORE PARKER; and yet, when all
hearts were full, almost to bursting, in view of this great
bereavement, the most eloquent words seemed poor and
common-place. Silence was more expressive than speech.

His estimate of Mr. Parker was an exalted one. He
regarded him as one of the most remarkable men the world
had ever seen — a prodigy as to his scholarly attainments,
and his power to acquire knowledge in all its varied forms,
which he dispensed with unbounded munificence for the en-
lightenment and elevation of his race. He felt very sad
at ·his departure, which he regarded as premature, the
result of overtasking his bodily powers, though for the
noblest ends. He thought his friend, Mr. Phillips, needed
to be admonished, rather than stimulated to more protracted
labors, by that light which he so often saw in Mr. Parker's
study, at the sacrifice of needed rest. It was not an example to be imitated, for it was using up life too rapidly, in
violation of physiological law. How often — even before
he saw any sign of failing health on the part of Mr. Parker
— had he warned him, with all earnestness, that, by such
unremitted studies and labors, he was surely "treasuring
up wrath against the day of wrath!" But he was wont
playfully, yet confidently, to refer to the longevity of his
ancestors as full security in his own case. His (Mr. G.'s)
reply was, "I do not doubt that your great-grandfather, and
grandfather, and father, were amply endowed with brains;
but they never used them as you are tasking yours; and
you must be more careful, or the penalty will come." Nevertheless, if Mr. Parker had fallen thus prematurely, it was
a rich consolation to know that it was the result of earnest
devotion to the cause of truth, freedom, and humanity, and
a very noble sacrifice indeed.

Mr. Garrison referred to the mental independence and

moral courage which characterized Mr. Parker in respect to all his convictions and acts. He was not, technically, "a Garrisonian Abolitionist," though often upon that platform, but voted with the Republican party, though faithfully rebuking it for its timidity and growing spirit of compromise. He was no man's man, and no man's follower, but acted for himself, bravely, conscientiously, and according to his best judgment.

But, what of his theology? Mr. Garrison did not know that he could state the whole of Mr. Parker's creed, but he remembered a part of it:— There is one God and Father over all, absolute and immutable, whose love is infinite, and therefore inexhaustible, and whose tender mercies are over all the works of his hand; and whether in the body, or out of the body, the farthest wanderer from the fold might yet have hope. He believed in the continual progress and final redemption of the human race; that every child of God, however erring, would ultimately be brought back. "You may quarrel with that theology," said Mr. Garrison, "if you please; I shall not. I like it; I have great faith in it; I accept it. But this I say, in respect to mere abstract theological opinions—the longer I live, the less do I care about them, the less do I make them a test of character. It is nothing to me that any man calls himself a Methodist, or Baptist, or Unitarian, or Universalist. These sectarian shibboleths are easily taken upon the lip, especially when the 'offence of the Cross' has ceased. Whoever will, with his theology, grind out the best grist for our common humanity, is the best theologian for me."

Many years ago, Thomas Jefferson uttered a sentiment which shocked our eminently *Christian* country as being thoroughly infidel: "I do not care," said he, "whether my neighbor believes in one God or in twenty gods, if he does not pick my pocket,"—thus going to the root of absolute justice and morality, and obviously meaning this : If a man pick my pocket, it is in vain he tells me, in palliation of his crime, "I am a believer in one living and true God." That may be, but you are a pickpocket, nevertheless. Or he may say, "I have not only one God, but twenty gods ; therefore, I am not guilty." Nay, but you are a thief! And so we always throw ourselves back upon character — upon the fact whether a man is honest, just, long-suffering, merciful ; and not whether he believes in a denominational creed, or is a strict observer of rites and ceremonies. This was the religion of Theodore Parker, — always exerting his marvellous powers to promote the common good, to bless those who needed a blessing, and to seek and to save the lost, to bear testimony in favor of the right, in the face of an ungodly age, and against " a frowning world."

Mr. Garrison said they were there to honor his memory. How could they best show their estimation of him? By trying to be like him in nobility of soul, in moral heroism, in fidelity to the truth, in disinterested regard for the welfare of others.

Mr. Parker, though strong in his convictions, was no dogmatist, and assumed no robes of infallibility. No man was more docile in regard to being taught, even by the lowliest. Mr. Phillips had done him no more than justice when he said, that he was willing and eager to obtain instruction from any quarter. Hence, he was always inquiring of those with whom he came in contact, so that he might learn, if possible, something from them that might aid him in the great work in which he was engaged.

When the question of Woman's Rights first came up for discussion, like multitudes of others, Mr. Parker was inclined to treat it facetiously, and supposed it could be put aside with a smile. Still, it was his disposition to hear and to learn ; and as soon as he began to investigate, and to see the grandeur and world-wide importance of the Woman's Rights movement, he gave to it his hearty support before the country and the world.

How he will be missed by those noble but unfortunate exiles who come to Boston from the old world, from time to time, driven out by the edicts of European despotism! What a home was Theodore Parker's for them! How they loved to gather around him in that home, and what a sympathizing friend, and trusty adviser, and generous assistant, in their times of sore distress, they have found in him! There are many such in Boston, and in various parts of our country, who have fled from foreign oppression, who will hear of his death with great sorrow of heart, and drop grateful tears to his memory.

Mr. President, our beloved friend and coadjutor has seen "the last of earth." We never shall behold his face again in the flesh. We shall never again hear the music of his voice, nor be inspired by his bodily presence. But is he dead? Are his great powers and faculties paralyzed? Is he now in inglorious rest? Or is he not, rather, more than ever before, alive, and beneficently at work? Is it a dream, a fiction of the brain, to believe that he really lives, and occupies a nobler and wider sphere, and that he will find a nobler and grander work to perform than he has been able to do here? I believe in immortal life,—not as a matter of logic or of metaphysics, for it does not come within the scope of these,—but I feel it in every fibre and nerve of my system, in every drop of my blood, in the very instinct, necessities, and desires of my nature.

> "The soul, secure in her existence, smiles
> At the drawn dagger, and defies its point."

This thought, in view of any mortal bereavement, however great, fills the soul with complete satisfaction, and inspires it with a new life.

> " God calls our loved ones, but we lose not wholly   ·
>   What He hath given ;
> They live on earth, in thought and deed, as truly
>   As in His heaven."

Our departed friend has left with us, and with mankind, his great thoughts and noble deeds, and they are imperishable. They have touched and quickened millions of minds already, and shall enlighten and inspire millions yet unborn ; and so, going down through the ages, they shall be a power to redeem mankind.

As for his reputation, so bitterly assailed and maliciously traduced while he lived, time will render it more and more illustrious. As for the stigmas cast upon him by narrow-minded bigots, and canting hypocrites, and craven time-servers, and cold-blooded conservatives, these are to give place to the plaudits of a discerning and an appreciating posterity. Thus it is that they who are willing to bear the cross are permitted in God's good time, to wear the crown !

> " For truth doth conquer at the last ;
>   So round and round we run ;
> And ever the right comes uppermost,
>   And ever is justice done ! "

REMARKS BY REV. JAMES FREEMAN CLARKE.

When I was asked if I also would say something here, I felt as our friend Wendell Phillips felt, and as our friend Mr. Garrison also felt, that this was not a time in which we could speak words which should analyze or describe the character of the man whose loss was filling our hearts with a sense of inexpressible grief; but, having heard them speak, some thoughts have come to me which I would like to utter.

We all have a feeling that Theodore Parker was the ripe and precious fruit of our New England soil, of our New England stock, of our New England mind, of our New England institutions. A better specimen of a full-grown, manly and womanly New England mind, heart and hand, has never ripened on these old gray rocks of Yankee land. How was he great? There are three directions in which a man may be great, and he was great in all three. There is the direction of the intellect. There are great thinkers; there are men who make themselves into a thinking machine; there are men who make themselves into a studying machine — who fill themselves full of all thoughts and all knowledges, and stop there. Theodore Parker had all the power of study that any of the hardest and ripest German students, who live for nothing but study, have had; but he had a great deal more. When he came back from his first journey to Europe, talking with me of the men whom he had seen in Germany, he said he went to see old Baur at Tubingen, and asked him how many hours he studied. He replied "Only eighteen hours;" but Baur was a student, and nothing but a student. Parker had studied his ten, twelve, and, for aught I know, his eighteen hours a day; but yet, all that was merely the beginning of what he was going to do with himself — merely the outside preparation for his after work. I remember meeting him on the cars on that fatal winter which laid the foundation of the disease which took him away. He had a carpet-bag with him, filled with German, Greek, and Latin books, — those old books, in vellum, of the seventeenth century, — volumes which it is a pain merely to look at, so hard reading do they seem to be. On

Monday morning, he filled his carpet-bag, and went to the place where he was to lecture Monday night; all day long he studied his books, and at night delivered his lecture. Then on Tuesday he would go to the next place, studying his books all day, and lecturing at night. So he would go on through the week, until Friday, when he would be back again to Boston, with his carpet-bag exhausted, with every one of those books gutted of its contents, with the whole substance of them in his brain, so that he knew all about every one of them, and could give a perfect analysis of them all, from beginning to end. On Saturday morning he would sit down to write his sermon for the next day; on Saturday afternoon go and visit the sick and bereaved of his society; on Sunday morning preach his sermon, and in the afternoon drive out to Watertown and preach there; and on Sunday evening he would lie on the sofa, and talk to his friends. That was his way of working. I got a letter, only yesterday, from William H. Channing, an old friend of his, who, speaking in the most tender and affectionate terms of his departure, said that he had, by over-working the intellectual part of his faculties, by too great fidelity in study, killed out, to some extent, another masterly faculty, which he had observed, but of which those who did not know him might be ignorant — namely, his gorgeous imagination. Mr. Channing said that he was a man who had, with all his logical power, with all those reflective faculties, with all those immense powers of grasp and reception, — the powers by which he held on to and retained what he had learned, and the powers by which he brought them into one great system, in order to set them before men, — with all this, he had the imagination of a poet, but did not let it work, he was so busy studying all the time.

Now, there were other students along with him when he was a boy, and I have known a great many students, but their way of studying was very different from his. When Parker studied, it was not merely with the concentration of certain faculties, for the sake of working out a certain problem, and there an end of it; or merely to gather together certain things and put them into his brain, and there an end of it No; he had a great idea before him all the time, and his study was always instinct with the life of that idea, and every word he uttered was a living word, and all the thoughts that came from him, came from him as fresh, glowing thoughts, — full of love to God and love to man.

Not to dwell on that, I say he was great, very great, intellectually, because he was not a narrow intellectual worker, but because he worked with the great reasoning faculty, which goes up to God the Eternal, at the same time that he worked with all those other intellectual powers which gathered together what God has sown broadcast over the earth, and by which he matured them for ripe and present use. When I saw him, on his return from Europe the last time, he told me of a long conversation which he had with a scholar at Oxford, I think, or Cambridge, who had lived for nothing but to study Aristotle; that was his business in the world — to know all about Aristotle; and Parker said that he discussed with him, through a whole summer day, Aristotle. When they had exhausted that subject, Parker asked him if he knew any thing about Plato. He said, "I have read Plato once;" and then Parker began upon Plato, and went through with every one of the dialogues, and taught him all he did not know about Plato. This is but a little part of Parker's knowledge, of which not one in ten thousand ever heard; and it is a specimen of the quantity and kind of knowledge which he had packed away ready for use.

Now, with regard to the second thing which goes to make a man great. What was Parker's way of action? It was a grand way of action. His activity was as large, determined, persistent, complete, and thorough as his intellectual working was. What he did was on a plan reaching through years — on a plan arranged when he was a boy; the whole of his life mapped out before him, with all he meant to do each year previously arranged, and the reason for it fixed in his own mind; and then he went to his work and did it — lived to accomplish it. But what sort of work was it? Greatness in work considers the quality of the work as well as the amount and method of accomplishing it. What was the quality of his work? It was simply this: it was to lift man toward God. That was the work which Parker gave himself to do in the world. That was the work for which he gathered together all this knowledge, that the work for which he so trained his intellect to be acute, persistent, and comprehensive. It was to raise men to God. With his eye on God, he turned to man to lift him up; and wherever he found a man who needed to be raised, or a class, a race, or a nation, that needed to be lifted up, there he felt his work to be. On that point I say no more, because it is the least necessary to speak of his work, since that is patent and known to all.

But there is one other element of greatness in man. Besides the head and the hand, there is the heart. What was the greatness of heart in Theodore Parker? His habit was in speaking of the Almighty, not to call Him the Almighty. He spoke of the "Absolute Father," in his philosophy and in his theology; but when he came to speak of Him from the pulpit, as a Christian man speaking to Christian men, as a brother talking to brethren and sisters of what they needed, it was "Father" and "Mother" — "the Great Father and Mother of us all." The tender, feminine heart of Theodore Parker was not satisfied with the name of "Father," unless he united with it that of "Mother." So tender was he, so affectionate was he, that no one was ever

5 *

near to Parker as a friend, as an intimate companion, without wondering how it was that men could ever think of him as hard, stern, severe, cold, and domineering, because, in all the private relations of life, he was as docile as a child to the touch of love, and it was only necessary, if you had any fault to find with any thing that he had said or done, to go to him and tell him just what your complaint was, or what your difficulty was, and just as likely as not he would at once admit, if there was the least reason in the complaint, that he was wrong. He was as ready to admit himself in the wrong as to maintain his stand for the everlasting right.

When Theodore Parker was about going away, and I went to see him for the last time, he followed me to the door of his study, and, putting his hands on my shoulders, he kissed my cheek, and said, "James, if you and I never meet again in this world, we have the happiness of knowing that there never has been between us one word, or one feeling, or one action, of unkindness." In the Old World, you will see men who carry in their button holes a red ribbon — the sign that they belong to the Legion of Honor. As long as I live, I shall carry (not apparent to others, but known to myself) the mark of that tender, fraternal kiss on my cheek. It is to me the sign of belonging to the Legion of Honor.

I do not know how to describe — with what figure borrowed from nature, or art, or history to describe — how Parker seems to me, in all this varied and accumulated greatness of mind, of heart, and of hand, better than by telling you the incidents of one day of my life. When I was passing out of Italy once, by the St. Gothard route, we were in Italy in the morning, on the Italian side of the mountains, surrounded by Italian voices, and by the music of Italian nightingales, and within sight of the opening vineyards. Then we began the ascent of the mountain, and as we ascended, we passed through the valley of pines, until at last, on that fifteenth day of May, we came to the snow. Then we took the little sleds, and went on upon the snow, higher and higher, until we were surrounded with great fields of snow, dazzling white in the sun; and on one side we saw the fall of a terrible avalanche, with its roar of thunder. So we passed on, until we reached the summit of the mountain, and then, descending on the other side, we came at last to where again the snow ceased, and there taking the diligence, we went on our way down the side of the mountain, through gorges and ravines, and glaciers even, the country around growing more and more green, changing from spring to summer, until at last, when we came down toward the Lake of Lucerne, we passed through orchards full of apple-blossoms, and finally crossed the beautiful lake to the town of Lucerne, there to receive a whole bundle of letters from home — from father, mother, brother, sister, and child — to end the day. When I think of that day's journey, beginning in Italy and ending in Germany, beginning under an Italian sun, at midday surrounded by snow-fields and glaciers, and at its close amid the apple-blossoms of Germany, it seems to me that that varied and wonderful day is a sort of type of the life of our friend THEODORE PARKER; its youth Italian — all fresh and gushing with ten thousand springs of early, boyish life and hope and animation, and with all the varied study and activity of the child and youth; its early morning passed in the stern work of climbing up the mountain side; its midday, with God's everlasting sun over his head, and the great, broad fields all around, over which his eye looked; and all through its afternoon hours, passing on into an ever-increasing affluence of spring and summer, and ending at last in the sweet bosom of affection, gratitude, and love.

How shall we miss him! The days are to come when we shall know how we miss him. When that great Hall stands closed and silent on the Lord's day, — empty and silent, because there is no one here who has the commanding ability which can bring together those great multitudes Sunday after Sunday, month after month, and year after year, to be taught and fed, — when great crises of the nation come, and pass unexamined, and not understood, because that great masterly power of analysis is taken from us, — when great national crimes are repeated again and again, and not rebuked to the listening ear of the nation, because there is no great power of intellect and knowledge adequate to that work — then we shall remember and feel and mourn the loss of THEODORE PARKER.

www.ingramcontent.com/pod-product-compliance
Lightning Source LLC
Chambersburg PA
CBHW021640270326
41931CB00008B/1098